CONTENTS

INTRODUCTION

Welcome to "The Simplified HubSpot User Guide" – your comprehensive companion to unlocking the full potential of one of the most powerful marketing and sales automation platforms available today. Whether you're a seasoned marketer or a business owner looking to revolutionize your customer engagement, this book is tailored to equip you with the knowledge and tools needed to thrive in the digital landscape.

In a world driven by data and technology, mastering the art of customer engagement and lead conversion has become essential for business success. HubSpot, a trailblazer in the realm of inbound marketing, offers an all-in-one solution that empowers organizations to attract, engage, and delight their audience effectively.

This user-friendly guide aims to demystify HubSpot and its array of features, making it accessible to users of all levels of experience. We will navigate through the platform step-by-step, unraveling its complexities, and presenting them in a straightforward manner. By the end of this journey, you will possess the knowledge and confidence to harness HubSpot's capabilities, optimize your marketing efforts, and elevate your sales performance.

Whether you're seeking to generate more qualified leads, automate repetitive tasks, track customer interactions, or measure the impact of your marketing campaigns

– this guide has you covered. From setting up your account to implementing advanced marketing automation workflows, you'll discover how HubSpot can become the engine that drives your business forward.

But this guide is more than just a technical manual; it's a testament to the power of innovation and adaptability in the digital age. As the marketing and sales landscapes evolve, so must our strategies and approaches. The world of HubSpot is dynamic, and this guide will equip you to stay agile in an ever-changing environment.

As we delve into the world of HubSpot together, embrace curiosity and a willingness to explore. Experiment with different techniques, and don't be afraid to challenge traditional marketing norms. Let this book be your springboard for creativity, as you discover new and exciting ways to connect with your audience and foster lasting relationships.

So, whether you're a marketing enthusiast, a business professional, or an aspiring entrepreneur, get ready to unlock the true potential of HubSpot. Let "The Simplified HubSpot User Guide" be your trusted companion on this transformative journey. Together, we'll empower your business to thrive, succeed, and stand out in an ever-evolving digital landscape. Let's embark on this adventure together!

CHAPTER ONE

Introduction to Hubspot

What is Hubspot?

Hubspot is a comprehensive, all-in-one inbound marketing, sales, and customer service platform designed to help businesses attract, engage, and delight customers. Founded in 2006 by Brian Halligan and Dharmesh Shah, Hubspot has grown into one of the leading customer relationship management (CRM) tools, catering to businesses of all sizes and industries.

At its core, Hubspot revolves around the concept of inbound marketing, which focuses on attracting potential customers through valuable content and personalized experiences rather than traditional interruptive advertising. The platform offers a suite of integrated tools and features that enable businesses to create, manage, and optimize their marketing, sales, and customer service efforts in a unified and efficient manner.

One of the key aspects that sets Hubspot apart is its user-friendly interface and the ability to automate and streamline various marketing and sales processes. From generating leads and managing marketing campaigns to tracking customer interactions and analyzing performance metrics, Hubspot offers a centralized hub for all these activities.

Key Features of Hubspot

To better understand the functionalities of Hubspot, let's explore some of its key features:

- Inbound Marketing Tools: Hubspot provides a range of tools to create and manage content, such as blog posts, landing pages, and social media posts. These tools aim to attract, convert, and engage visitors into potential leads.
- CRM (Customer Relationship Management): The CRM tool helps businesses organize and track interactions with leads and customers. It allows teams to manage contact information, communication history, and deals in one place.
- Marketing Automation: Hubspot's automation capabilities enable marketers to schedule emails, segment leads based on behaviors, and nurture leads with personalized content.
- Sales Hub: The Sales Hub assists sales teams in managing leads, automating tasks, and tracking the sales pipeline to close deals effectively.
- Service Hub: This feature allows businesses to provide exceptional customer service by tracking and resolving customer inquiries through various channels, like email and live chat.
- Reporting and Analytics: Hubspot offers powerful analytics and reporting tools, enabling businesses to measure the success of their marketing campaigns, sales efforts, and customer service interactions.

Integration Capabilities

Another aspect that adds to Hubspot's appeal is its ability to integrate with various third-party tools and software. This integration capability enhances the platform's functionality, allowing businesses to sync data between applications, streamline processes, and gain deeper insights.

Hubspot integrates with popular tools like Salesforce, Gmail, Microsoft Office, and numerous e-commerce platforms. This enables businesses to maintain a seamless workflow across different systems, ensuring data consistency and efficiency across the organization.

Benefits of Using Hubspot

Using Hubspot can provide numerous advantages for businesses looking to scale their marketing, sales, and customer service efforts. Let's delve into some of the key benefits:

- Time Efficiency: With all essential marketing, sales, and service tools integrated into a single platform, Hubspot saves businesses valuable time and effort. Teams can access and manage their tasks from a centralized location, eliminating the need to switch between multiple tools and reducing administrative overhead.
- Enhanced Customer Experience: Hubspot's focus on inbound marketing and personalization helps businesses provide a better customer experience. By understanding customer needs and interests, companies can deliver targeted content and tailor interactions, ultimately building stronger and more meaningful relationships.
- Increased Lead Generation: The inbound

marketing tools in Hubspot allow businesses to attract leads organically through valuable content and SEO strategies. The platform's landing page and lead capture features enable effective lead generation and conversion.

- Data-Driven Decision Making: Hubspot's robust reporting and analytics capabilities offer valuable insights into marketing, sales, and customer service performance. Businesses can track key metrics, identify trends, and make data-driven decisions to optimize their strategies.
- Scalability: Hubspot caters to businesses of all sizes, from startups to large enterprises. As companies grow, Hubspot's flexible plans and scalable features ensure that the platform can accommodate their evolving needs and demands.
- Streamlined Collaboration: Hubspot fosters better collaboration between marketing, sales, and service teams. With shared access to customer data and communication history, teams can work cohesively to provide a seamless customer experience.
- Automation and Personalization: The automation features of Hubspot enable businesses to automate repetitive tasks, such as email follow-ups and lead nurturing. Simultaneously, the platform's personalization capabilities allow for targeted messaging and content, leading to higher engagement and conversion rates.

Getting Started with Hubspot

Getting started with Hubspot is a straightforward process. Businesses can sign up for a free trial or choose from various subscription plans based on their specific needs. Let's break down the steps to begin using Hubspot effectively:

- Account Creation: To begin, visit the Hubspot website and sign up for an account. During the signup process, you will need to provide some basic information about your business and your goals with Hubspot.
- Onboarding and Setup: Once your account is created, Hubspot will guide you through the onboarding process. You'll be asked to define your marketing, sales, and service goals, and set up the necessary integrations with existing tools and platforms.
- Familiarizing with the Interface: After completing the initial setup, take some time to explore the Hubspot dashboard and interface. Familiarize yourself with the different sections and tools available, as this will be the central hub for your marketing, sales, and service activities.
- Importing Data: If you have an existing CRM or customer data, you can import it into Hubspot to ensure a smooth transition. This will allow you to continue managing your customer relationships without any disruption.
- Setting Up Workflows: Workflows are essential for automating various processes within Hubspot. Create workflows to automate lead nurturing, follow-up emails, and other repetitive tasks, freeing up time for your team to focus on high-value activities.
- Content Creation: Utilize Hubspot's content creation tools to build engaging blog posts,

landing pages, and email campaigns. Remember to optimize your content for SEO to attract more organic traffic.

- Lead Capture and Management: Implement lead capture forms and landing pages to collect visitor information and manage leads effectively within the Hubspot CRM.
- Training and Support: Hubspot provides a wealth of training resources and a supportive community to help users make the most of the platform. Take advantage of webinars, tutorials, and documentation to enhance your understanding of Hubspot's capabilities.

Navigating the Hubspot Dashboard

The Hubspot dashboard is the central command center where users can access all of the platform's features and tools. Navigating the dashboard efficiently is crucial for managing marketing, sales, and service activities effectively. Let's explore the main components of the Hubspot dashboard:

- Home: The home tab provides an overview of your account's performance, including website traffic, lead conversion rates, and recent activities. It serves as a snapshot of your business's overall health.
- Marketing: The marketing tab is where you'll find all the tools and features related to inbound marketing. This includes creating and managing blog posts, landing pages, email campaigns, social media publishing, and SEO optimization.
- Sales: In the sales tab, you can access tools for

managing your sales pipeline, tracking deals, and communicating with leads and customers. This section also includes automation features for streamlining sales processes.

- Service: The service tab is dedicated to customer service and support. Here, you can manage and track customer inquiries, set up a knowledge base, and use live chat to assist customers in real-time.
- Reports: The reports tab is where you can access in-depth analytics and performance metrics for your marketing, sales, and service efforts. Utilize these insights to measure success, identify areas for improvement, and make data-driven decisions.
- Automation: The automation tab houses the workflows and automation settings. This is where you can create, manage, and analyze automated processes to streamline repetitive tasks and improve efficiency.
- Settings: The settings tab allows you to customize your Hubspot account, including user permissions, email preferences, and integration settings with other tools and platforms.

Hubspot's dashboard is designed to be intuitive and user-friendly, making it easy for users to access the necessary tools and data quickly. By effectively navigating the dashboard, businesses can leverage Hubspot's capabilities to drive growth, increase customer satisfaction, and achieve their marketing and sales objectives.

In conclusion, Hubspot is a powerful platform that offers a wealth of features to help businesses attract, engage, and delight customers through inbound marketing, sales, and customer service efforts. Its user-friendly interface, integration capabilities, and comprehensive functionalities make it a valuable asset for organizations seeking to streamline their operations and drive sustainable growth. By harnessing the benefits of Hubspot and mastering the navigation of its dashboard, businesses can pave the way for success in the dynamic and competitive digital landscape.

Setting Up Your Hubspot Account

Creating Your Hubspot Account

Creating a Hubspot account is the first step towards harnessing the power of this comprehensive inbound marketing and CRM platform. Follow the steps below to set up your account:

- Go to the Hubspot Website: Visit the official Hubspot website (www.hubspot.com) and click on the "Get Hubspot Free" or "Get Started" button, depending on the available options.
- Sign Up: You'll be prompted to sign up with your email address. You can also sign up using your Google account or Microsoft Office 365 credentials for added convenience.
- Provide Business Information: Once you've entered your email, you'll need to provide some basic information about your business, such as its name, industry, and website URL.
- Set Up Goals: Hubspot will ask you about your primary marketing, sales, and customer service goals. This information helps the platform customize your experience and recommend relevant tools.
- Choose Your Plan: After completing the initial setup, you'll be given options for various plans. Hubspot offers different tiers to accommodate businesses of all sizes, including a free plan with limited features and paid plans with additional capabilities.
- Verify Your Account: Depending on your chosen

plan and country regulations, Hubspot may require you to verify your account by providing additional information or confirming your email.

- Welcome to Hubspot: Congratulations! You've successfully created your Hubspot account. Now, you can start exploring the platform and setting up your marketing, sales, and service activities.

Integrating Your CRM and Other Tools

Integrating your CRM and other tools with Hubspot is essential to centralize data, improve efficiency, and maintain consistency across different systems. Hubspot offers a wide range of integrations with popular third-party tools. Here's how to integrate your CRM and other tools with Hubspot:

- CRM Integration: If you already have a CRM system in place, such as Salesforce or Microsoft Dynamics, you can seamlessly integrate it with Hubspot. Go to the "Settings" tab in your Hubspot dashboard and select "Integrations." Look for your CRM provider and follow the step-by-step instructions to set up the integration.
- Email Integration: Hubspot can sync with your email provider (e.g., Gmail, Outlook) to track email interactions automatically. This integration helps you log emails, schedule follow-ups, and access templates directly from your email interface.
- Social Media Integration: Connect your social media accounts to Hubspot to manage and schedule posts, track engagement, and measure the impact of your social media efforts.

- Marketing Automation Integration: If you use marketing automation tools like Zapier or Automate.io, you can integrate them with Hubspot to streamline workflows and automate repetitive tasks.
- E-commerce Integration: If your business operates an e-commerce platform like Shopify or Magento, integrating it with Hubspot enables you to track customer behavior, monitor purchase history, and run targeted marketing campaigns.
- Content Management System (CMS) Integration: If you have a CMS like WordPress or Drupal, integrating it with Hubspot ensures seamless content publishing and tracking of website visitors and leads.
- Analytics and Reporting Integration: Connect Hubspot with tools like Google Analytics or Data Studio to consolidate data and gain deeper insights into your marketing and sales performance.

Hubspot's extensive integration capabilities make it a versatile platform that can work cohesively with your existing tools, enhancing your overall marketing and sales efficiency.

Customizing Your Dashboard and Settings

Customizing your Hubspot dashboard and settings allows you to tailor the platform to your specific business needs and preferences. Here are some key areas to focus on for a personalized experience:

- Dashboard Layout: The Hubspot dashboard is customizable, allowing you to arrange widgets and data cards to suit your preferences. Click on the "Customize" or "Edit Layout" option on the dashboard to drag and drop widgets into different positions, or add new widgets relevant to your goals.

- User Permissions: In the settings tab, you can manage user permissions to control access to various features and data within Hubspot. Assign roles and permissions based on team members' responsibilities to ensure data security and streamlined collaboration.
- Email Settings: Customize your email settings to reflect your brand identity. You can upload your company logo, set default email signatures, and configure other email-related preferences.
- Contact Properties: Define custom contact properties that align with your business needs. These properties allow you to store and organize specific information about your contacts for better segmentation and personalization.
- Workflows and Automation: Set up workflows to automate tasks and actions based on predefined criteria. Customizing workflows allows you to create personalized experiences for leads and customers at different stages of the buyer's journey.
- Reporting Dashboards: Create custom reporting dashboards to monitor the key metrics that matter most to your business. This will enable you to keep a close eye on your marketing, sales, and service performance and make informed decisions accordingly.
- Notifications and Reminders: Configure

notifications and reminders for essential tasks and follow-ups. This will help you stay on top of your marketing and sales activities and ensure timely responses to customer inquiries.

- Language and Timezone Settings: If your business operates in multiple regions or countries, adjust the language and timezone settings to provide a seamless experience for your global audience.

By customizing your dashboard and settings, you can optimize Hubspot to align with your business goals and workflows, creating a more efficient and tailored experience for your team. Take the time to explore the various customization options and make the most out of Hubspot's flexibility and adaptability.

In summary, creating your Hubspot account is a straightforward process that involves signing up, providing business information, and choosing the right plan for your needs. Integrating your CRM and other tools with Hubspot centralizes data and improves efficiency across different systems. Customizing your dashboard and settings allows you to tailor the platform to your specific requirements, making it a more powerful and personalized tool for your marketing, sales, and customer service efforts. With a fully configured Hubspot account, you can unlock the platform's full potential and drive business growth through inbound marketing and exceptional customer experiences.

Managing Contacts In Hubspot

Importing and Organizing Contacts

Importing and organizing contacts is a critical step in leveraging the power of HubSpot's CRM and marketing tools. Properly managing your contacts ensures that you can effectively engage with leads and customers, deliver targeted content, and nurture relationships. Here's how you can import and organize contacts in HubSpot:

- Importing Contacts: To import contacts into HubSpot, go to the "Contacts" tab in your dashboard and click on "Import." You can choose to upload a CSV file or import contacts from other sources like Gmail or Outlook. Make sure that your contact data is clean and well-structured before importing to avoid duplicates or errors.
- Organizing Contacts with Lists: After importing your contacts, create lists to categorize them based on specific criteria. For instance, you can create lists for leads, customers, prospects, or based on demographic information. Lists help you segment your contacts and target them with personalized marketing campaigns.
- Using Smart Lists: HubSpot offers Smart Lists, which are dynamic lists that automatically update based on predefined conditions. For example, you can create a Smart List for leads who have visited specific website pages or engaged with certain email campaigns.
- Adding Contacts to Workflows: Once your contacts are organized into lists, you can add

them to workflows for automated nurturing. Workflows enable you to send targeted emails, set follow-up tasks for your sales team, and move contacts through the sales funnel.

- Cleaning and Updating Contacts: Regularly review and update your contacts to ensure accurate and up-to-date information. HubSpot provides tools to deduplicate contacts and merge duplicate records, maintaining a clean and organized database.
- Integrating with Form Submissions: Integrate your website's lead capture forms with HubSpot to automatically add new contacts to your CRM. This ensures a seamless flow of data and prevents manual data entry errors.
- Utilizing Contact Insights: Take advantage of HubSpot's contact insights to gain a deeper understanding of your leads and customers. Track their interactions with your website, emails, and content to tailor your marketing efforts.

Segmentation and List Management

Segmentation is a powerful marketing strategy that involves dividing your audience into distinct groups based on specific characteristics or behaviors. It allows you to deliver personalized and relevant content to each segment, increasing engagement and conversion rates. HubSpot provides robust tools for segmentation and list management:

- Defining Segmentation Criteria: Determine the criteria you'll use to segment your contacts. This can include factors like location, industry, job title, engagement level, or any other relevant data points.

- Creating Static Lists: Static lists are manually curated and don't change unless contacts are added or removed manually. Use static lists for specific one-time campaigns or to target a particular subset of contacts.
- Using Smart Lists: As mentioned earlier, Smart Lists are dynamic and automatically update based on predefined conditions. Use Smart Lists to target contacts based on their behavior, such as those who opened specific emails or downloaded particular resources.
- Employing Custom Properties: Utilize custom contact properties to collect and store additional information about your contacts. For example, you can create a property for "Preferred Communication Channel" to tailor your communication accordingly.
- Building Segmented Campaigns: When creating email or marketing campaigns, choose the relevant lists or segments to target. This ensures that your messages are more relevant to the recipients, leading to higher engagement and conversion rates.
- A/B Testing Segments: To optimize your marketing efforts, consider conducting A/B tests with different segments. Test various messaging, offers, or content to identify the most effective approach for each segment.
- Analyzing Segment Performance: Regularly analyze the performance of your segmented campaigns. Measure open rates, click-through

rates, and conversion rates for each segment to refine your segmentation strategy further.

Segmentation empowers you to deliver personalized and targeted content, which leads to higher customer satisfaction and better marketing results.

Creating and Using Contact Properties

Contact properties are attributes or data points that provide essential information about your contacts. Creating and using contact properties in HubSpot enables you to collect and organize relevant data, personalize communication, and tailor your marketing and sales efforts. Here's how to create and use contact properties effectively:

- Assessing Information Needs: Before creating contact properties, determine the information you need to collect and store about your contacts. Consider demographic data (e.g., name, company, job title), engagement data (e.g., email opens, website visits), and any other relevant details.
- Creating Custom Properties: In the "Contacts" tab, click on "Manage" and then select "Properties." Click on "Create Property" and choose the appropriate type, such as text, date, or dropdown. Name the property and define its options or values if applicable.
- Mapping Fields during Import: When importing contacts, map the fields from your CSV file to the corresponding contact properties in HubSpot. This ensures that the data is correctly populated in your CRM.
- Personalizing Emails and Content: Use contact

properties to personalize your email campaigns and content. For example, address contacts by their first name, or tailor content based on their industry or preferences.

- Customizing Workflows: Leverage contact properties in your workflows to trigger specific actions or email sequences based on specific criteria. This helps automate personalized communication and lead nurturing.
- Updating Properties Regularly: Regularly update contact properties as new information becomes available. This ensures that your data remains accurate and relevant.
- Creating Smart Lists with Properties: Use contact properties as criteria when creating Smart Lists. This allows you to segment contacts dynamically based on specific attributes or behaviors.

By utilizing contact properties effectively, you can build a comprehensive profile of your contacts and deliver personalized experiences that resonate with them.

Tracking Contact Activity and Interaction

Tracking contact activity and interaction is essential for understanding your audience's behavior, preferences, and engagement level. HubSpot offers various tools to monitor contact activities, helping you optimize your marketing and sales efforts. Here's how to track contact activity effectively:

- Email Tracking: HubSpot's email tracking feature allows you to see when contacts open your emails and click on links. Use this data to gauge engagement and follow up with interested leads promptly.

- Website Tracking: Integrate HubSpot's tracking code into your website to monitor contact activity. Track page visits, form submissions, and other interactions to gain insights into how leads engage with your website.
- Content Engagement: HubSpot provides data on how contacts engage with your content, such as blog posts, eBooks, and videos. Analyze this information to identify which content resonates most with your audience.
- Event Tracking: Use custom event tracking to monitor specific actions taken by contacts, such as downloading a resource, registering for a webinar, or attending an event. This data helps you assess lead interest and engagement.
- Lead Scoring: Implement lead scoring to assign a numerical value to contacts based on their activities and interactions. This system helps prioritize leads and identify those who are most likely to convert into customers.
- Interaction History: HubSpot's CRM stores the interaction history of each contact, allowing you to view past engagements and communications. This helps your sales team have informed conversations with leads.
- Analyzing Activity Reports: Regularly review activity reports to identify trends and patterns in contact behavior. Use this information to refine your marketing and sales strategies.

Tracking contact activity empowers you to deliver relevant and timely content, engage leads effectively, and tailor your sales approach based on customer interactions.

By leveraging HubSpot's tracking capabilities, you can enhance your understanding of your audience and create more personalized experiences that drive results.

In conclusion, effectively managing and organizing contacts in HubSpot is essential for successful marketing and sales efforts. By importing and organizing contacts, utilizing segmentation and list management, creating and using contact properties, and tracking contact activity and interactions, businesses can build strong relationships with leads and customers. These practices, combined with HubSpot's powerful features and tools, enable businesses to optimize their marketing, sales, and customer service strategies for sustainable growth and success.

CHAPTER TWO

Understanding Hubspot's
Marketing Tools

Creating and Managing Email Campaigns

Email marketing is a powerful tool for engaging with leads and customers, nurturing relationships, and driving conversions. With HubSpot's email marketing tools, creating and managing effective email campaigns becomes a seamless process. Here's how to make the most of HubSpot's capabilities for email marketing:

- Email Templates: HubSpot offers a variety of pre-designed email templates that are customizable to match your brand's look and feel. You can also create your own custom templates for consistent branding across all communications.
- Personalization: Utilize contact properties to personalize your email content. Address recipients by their names and tailor the content based on their preferences, behaviors, or demographics.
- Segmentation: Use the lists and Smart Lists created earlier to segment your contacts. This allows you to send targeted emails to specific groups based on their interests and engagement levels.

- A/B Testing: Experiment with different email subject lines, content, or calls-to-action using HubSpot's A/B testing feature. This helps you identify the most effective elements to optimize your email campaigns.
- Automated Workflows: Set up email workflows to automate lead nurturing and follow-up sequences based on specific triggers or time intervals. This saves time and ensures timely and relevant communications.
- Monitoring Engagement: Track email open rates, click-through rates, and conversion rates to gauge the effectiveness of your email campaigns. Use these insights to refine your email marketing strategy.
- Email Sequences: Use email sequences to deliver a series of emails to contacts over a period of time. This is particularly useful for onboarding new customers or guiding leads through a sales funnel.

Designing Landing Pages and Forms

Landing pages and forms are vital elements for capturing leads and driving conversions. HubSpot provides user-friendly tools for designing and optimizing landing pages and forms. Here's how to create compelling landing pages and forms in HubSpot:

- Landing Page Templates: HubSpot offers a range of professionally designed landing page templates. Choose a template that aligns with your campaign goals and customize it to suit your needs.
- Clear and Concise Content: Keep your landing

page content clear, concise, and focused on the value proposition. Use persuasive copy, images, and videos to encourage visitors to take the desired action.

- Mobile Responsiveness: Ensure that your landing pages are mobile-responsive, as a significant portion of website traffic comes from mobile devices. HubSpot's templates automatically adjust to various screen sizes.
- Smart Forms: Use HubSpot's Smart Forms to display different questions to visitors based on their previous interactions with your website. This helps prevent form fatigue and improves the user experience.
- Progressive Profiling: Implement progressive profiling to collect additional information from repeat visitors. Gradually gather more data over time to build a comprehensive profile without overwhelming leads.
- Thank You Pages: Design engaging thank you pages that follow the conversion. Include relevant content or a call-to-action to keep the momentum going and encourage further engagement.
- A/B Testing: Test different elements of your landing pages and forms, such as headlines, images, or form fields, to optimize conversion rates. HubSpot's built-in A/B testing feature makes this process easy.

Implementing Lead Capture and Conversion Strategies

To maximize lead capture and conversion rates, consider implementing the following strategies using HubSpot:

- Lead Magnets: Offer valuable lead magnets such as eBooks, whitepapers, or webinars in exchange for contact information. Use HubSpot to deliver these resources automatically upon form submission.
- Call-to-Action (CTA) Optimization: Design compelling CTAs that stand out and encourage visitors to take action. HubSpot allows you to create and track CTAs to identify which ones perform best.
- Pop-Up Forms: Use pop-up forms to capture leads at strategic points on your website. However, be mindful of user experience and ensure that pop-ups appear at appropriate times.
- Exit-Intent Pop-Ups: Implement exit-intent pop-ups to capture leads from visitors who are about to leave your website. Offer discounts, content, or incentives to entice them to stay.
- Lead Scoring and Nurturing: Assign lead scores based on engagement level and interactions with your content. Use lead nurturing workflows to send targeted emails and content based on lead behavior.
- Chatbots and Live Chat: Utilize HubSpot's chatbot and live chat features to engage with website visitors in real-time. This allows you to address queries, provide support, and capture leads more effectively.
- Social Media Lead Ads: Integrate HubSpot with your social media platforms to capture leads directly from social media lead ads. This streamlines lead generation and ensures that leads are automatically added to your CRM.

Leveraging HubSpot's Blogging and SEO Features

Blogging and SEO play a crucial role in attracting organic traffic and increasing visibility in search engine results. HubSpot offers powerful tools to help you optimize your blog posts and improve your search engine rankings. Here's how to leverage HubSpot's blogging and SEO features effectively:

- Content Strategy: Plan your content strategy around relevant topics and keywords that align with your target audience's interests and pain points.
- Blogging Platform: Use HubSpot's built-in blogging platform to create and publish blog posts directly on your website. This streamlines content management and ensures that all your marketing efforts are centralized.
- SEO Optimization: Optimize your blog posts for search engines by incorporating target keywords, meta descriptions, and relevant tags. HubSpot's SEO recommendations feature provides insights to improve your content's searchability.
- Topic Clusters: Organize your blog content into topic clusters, where each cluster centers around a core topic and its related subtopics. This helps search engines understand the relevance and depth of your content.
- Internal Linking: Implement internal linking within your blog posts to guide readers to related content on your website. This not only improves user experience but also enhances SEO.
- Social Sharing: Enable social sharing buttons on your blog posts to encourage readers to share your

content on their social media networks. This helps increase your content's reach and visibility.

- Content Analytics: Utilize HubSpot's content analytics to track the performance of your blog posts, including views, engagement, and conversions. This data helps you identify high-performing content and areas for improvement.

By effectively utilizing HubSpot's email marketing, landing page and form design, lead capture and conversion strategies, blogging, and SEO features, businesses can enhance their online presence, engage with their audience, and drive meaningful results in their marketing efforts. HubSpot's all-in-one platform streamlines these processes, allowing businesses to focus on delivering exceptional experiences to their leads and customers.

Mastering Social Media Management

Connecting Your Social Media Accounts

HubSpot offers seamless integration with various social media platforms, enabling businesses to manage their social media presence from a centralized location. Connecting your social media accounts to HubSpot is a straightforward process. Here's how you can do it:

- Navigate to Social Media Settings: In your HubSpot dashboard, go to the "Marketing" tab and click on "Social" in the left-hand menu. Then, select "Social Settings."
- Add Social Media Accounts: Click on the "Connect Account" button to add your social media accounts. HubSpot supports integration with popular platforms like Facebook, Twitter, LinkedIn, Instagram, and more.
- Authorize Access: Follow the on-screen prompts to authorize HubSpot to access your social media accounts. This allows HubSpot to post on your behalf and collect social media data for analytics.
- Social Media Streams: After connecting your accounts, you'll see social media streams in the "Social" section. These streams display your social media activity and engagement in real-time.

Scheduling and Publishing Social Media Posts

With HubSpot's social media publishing tools, you can schedule and publish social media posts in advance, streamlining your social media management. Here's how to schedule and publish social media posts in HubSpot:

- Compose a Post: In the "Social" section, click on "Compose Post" to start creating your social media post. You can add text, images, videos, and links to your post.
- Select Social Media Channels: Choose the social media channels where you want to publish the post. You can select multiple platforms simultaneously.
- Schedule the Post: Click on the arrow next to the "Publish" button to access the scheduling options. Choose the date and time you want the post to go live and click "Schedule."
- Review and Manage Scheduled Posts: You can view and manage all your scheduled posts in the "Scheduled" tab. From here, you can edit, reschedule, or delete posts as needed.
- Social Campaigns: HubSpot allows you to group related posts into social campaigns. This helps you organize and track the performance of your social media efforts effectively.
- Monitor Post Engagement: After posts are published, you can track their engagement metrics, such as likes, comments, shares, and clicks, within the "Social" section.

Monitoring and Engaging with Social Media Interactions

HubSpot's social media monitoring tools enable businesses to keep track of social media interactions, mentions, and comments. Engaging with your audience on social media is crucial for building relationships and fostering brand loyalty. Here's how to monitor and engage with social media interactions in HubSpot:

- Social Media Streams: In the "Social" section, you'll find social media streams that display your accounts' activity and interactions. These streams allow you to monitor mentions, comments, and direct messages in real-time.
- Respond to Interactions: Engage with your audience by responding to comments and messages directly from the social media streams in HubSpot. Timely responses show that you value customer feedback and actively engage with your followers.
- Social Media Monitoring: Set up social media monitoring for specific keywords or mentions related to your brand or industry. This allows you to track conversations and join relevant discussions.
- Social Media Inbox: HubSpot's social media inbox aggregates all your social media interactions, mentions, and comments in one place. This simplifies social media management and ensures that no engagement goes unnoticed.

Analyzing Social Media Performance

Analyzing social media performance is essential for understanding the impact of your social media efforts and refining your social media strategy. HubSpot provides valuable analytics to measure the effectiveness of your social media campaigns. Here's how to analyze social media performance in HubSpot:

- Social Media Reports: In the "Social" section, click on "Reports" to access social media analytics. HubSpot provides a range of reports, including post performance, audience insights, and social interactions.

- Post Performance: Analyze the performance of your social media posts, including reach, engagement, and click-through rates. Identify which posts resonate most with your audience and replicate successful content.
- Audience Insights: Use audience insights to understand the demographics, interests, and behaviors of your social media followers. This information helps you tailor your content to better suit your target audience.
- Social Media Interactions: Track the interactions and engagement your social media accounts receive over time. This data highlights trends and allows you to identify areas for improvement.
- Competitor Analysis: HubSpot's social media reports enable you to compare your social media performance with that of your competitors. Gain valuable insights and benchmark your efforts against industry leaders.
- Conversion Tracking: If you have HubSpot's marketing automation tools integrated with your website, you can track social media conversions. Measure the number of leads generated and customers acquired from social media campaigns.
- Reporting Frequency: Regularly review your social media reports to track progress and identify areas for optimization. Set up custom reports to receive updates on social media performance at regular intervals.

By connecting your social media accounts, scheduling and publishing social media posts, monitoring and engaging with social media interactions, and analyzing social media performance using HubSpot's robust tools, businesses can effectively manage their social media presence and drive meaningful results from their social media marketing efforts. HubSpot's all-in-one platform simplifies social media management, allowing businesses to focus on building strong relationships with their audience and achieving their marketing goals.

Creating Effective Marketing Automation

Understanding Workflows and Automation

Workflows and automation are essential components of a successful marketing strategy, streamlining repetitive tasks and nurturing leads through the buyer's journey. In HubSpot, workflows are sequences of automated actions triggered by specific events or conditions. Understanding how workflows and automation function is crucial for optimizing your marketing efforts. Here's a breakdown of workflows and automation in HubSpot:

- Trigger Events: Workflows are initiated by trigger events, such as a contact submitting a form, reaching a specific lead score, or interacting with certain content. These triggers define when the workflow should start.
- Actions and Conditions: Within a workflow, you can set up various actions and conditions. Actions are the steps that occur when a contact meets the trigger event, such as sending an email or updating a contact property. Conditions determine the path a contact takes within the workflow based on their behavior or attributes.
- Goal and Enrollment Triggers: Workflows have a goal, which is the desired outcome, such as a completed purchase or a lead becoming an opportunity. Enrollment triggers determine how contacts are added to the workflow and when they exit it after completing the desired goal.
- Lead Nurturing: Workflows are powerful tools for lead nurturing, allowing you to deliver targeted

content at the right time based on a contact's behavior and interests.

- Sales and Service Automation: Workflows are not limited to marketing; they can also automate sales and customer service processes, such as sending follow-up emails, assigning tasks to sales representatives, or updating customer records.

Designing and Implementing Automated Workflows

Designing and implementing effective workflows is a strategic process that requires thoughtful planning and testing. To create successful automated workflows in HubSpot, consider the following steps:

- Define Goals and Objectives: Start by setting clear goals for your workflows. Identify the outcomes you want to achieve, such as lead nurturing, customer onboarding, or re-engagement campaigns.
- Identify Trigger Events: Determine the trigger events that will initiate the workflow. This could be a form submission, email interaction, specific website visit, or any other relevant behavior.
- Map the Workflow: Design the flow of the workflow, including the actions and conditions at each stage. Consider different paths based on the contacts' behavior to ensure a personalized experience.
- Create Personalized Content: Develop engaging and personalized content for each step of the workflow. Leverage dynamic content to customize the messaging based on contact attributes.
- Test and Optimize: Before launching the

workflow, thoroughly test it to ensure all actions and conditions are functioning as intended. Continuously monitor and optimize the workflow based on performance data.

- Enrollment Triggers: Choose the appropriate enrollment triggers to add contacts to the workflow. For example, you may want to enroll contacts based on specific properties, activities, or interactions.
- Set Goals and Exit Criteria: Define the goals of the workflow and the exit criteria for contacts who have completed the desired actions. This ensures that contacts progress through the workflow efficiently.
- Monitor Performance: Regularly review the performance of your automated workflows. Analyze metrics such as open rates, click-through rates, and conversion rates to identify areas for improvement.

Personalization and Dynamic Content in Automation

Personalization is key to delivering a relevant and engaging experience to your contacts. HubSpot's dynamic content feature allows you to customize content based on individual attributes, ensuring a more personalized journey for each contact. Here's how to leverage personalization and dynamic content in automation:

- Contact Properties: Utilize the contact properties you've collected to personalize your content. Address contacts by their first names, tailor content based on their industry, or any other relevant attribute.

- Smart Content: HubSpot's smart content feature allows you to show different content blocks to contacts based on their characteristics or behaviors. For example, you can display specific offers to leads at different stages of the sales funnel.
- Email Personalization: Personalize your email content by inserting contact properties into the subject line, greeting, and body of the email. This creates a more personalized and human touch in your communication.
- Dynamic Lists: Leverage dynamic lists to automatically segment contacts based on their actions, attributes, or behavior. These lists update dynamically as contacts meet the defined criteria.
- Dynamic Landing Pages: Customize landing pages using dynamic content based on the information you have about the visitor. Show relevant content that aligns with their interests and preferences.
- Tailored Call-to-Action (CTA): Use personalized CTAs that change based on the contact's attributes or stage in the buyer's journey. This encourages higher engagement and increases the chances of conversion.
- Behavioral Triggers: Implement behavioral triggers in your workflows to respond to contacts' actions in real-time. For example, if a contact abandons their shopping cart, you can send a follow-up email with personalized content.
- Progressive Profiling: Gradually collect additional information from contacts over time using progressive profiling. This prevents overwhelming visitors with too many form fields

and enhances the user experience.

By incorporating personalization and dynamic content into your automated workflows, you can deliver relevant and tailored experiences that resonate with your contacts. This leads to increased engagement, higher conversion rates, and improved customer satisfaction.

In conclusion, understanding workflows and automation is crucial for streamlining marketing, sales, and customer service processes. Designing and implementing effective workflows in HubSpot involves setting clear goals, identifying trigger events, mapping the workflow, and creating personalized content. Leveraging personalization and dynamic content in automation enhances the user experience, increases engagement, and drives better results from your marketing efforts. HubSpot's robust automation tools provide businesses with the capability to deliver personalized experiences at scale, driving growth and success in a competitive market.

Analyzing Your Marketing Performance

Tracking and Analyzing Website Traffic

Tracking and analyzing website traffic is essential for understanding how visitors interact with your website and identifying opportunities for improvement. HubSpot offers robust analytics tools that provide valuable insights into your website's performance. Here's how to track and analyze website traffic in HubSpot:

- HubSpot Tracking Code: Install HubSpot's tracking code on your website to start collecting data on visitor behavior. The tracking code records information such as page views, form submissions, and conversions.
- Website Analytics Dashboard: In your HubSpot dashboard, go to the "Reports" tab and select "Website Analytics." Here, you'll find a comprehensive overview of your website's performance, including total visits, new contacts, and conversion rates.
- Traffic Sources: Analyze the sources of your website traffic, such as organic search, social media, email campaigns, and direct visits. This data helps you understand which channels drive the most traffic and which areas need improvement.
- Page Performance: Examine the performance of individual web pages using the "Page Performance" report. Identify high-performing pages and those that may require optimization to improve user engagement.

- Conversion Funnel: Set up conversion funnels to track the steps visitors take on your website before completing a specific goal, such as filling out a contact form or making a purchase. Analyze funnel drop-offs to identify potential barriers in the user journey.
- Heatmaps and User Recordings: Utilize HubSpot's heatmaps and user recordings to visualize how visitors interact with your web pages. Heatmaps show where visitors click, scroll, and spend the most time, while user recordings provide real-time playback of individual visitor sessions.
- Mobile Performance: Assess the performance of your website on mobile devices using the "Mobile Performance" report. Ensure that your website is mobile-responsive and provides a seamless experience for mobile users.
- A/B Testing: Conduct A/B tests on various website elements, such as headlines, images, or calls-to-action, to optimize conversion rates and user engagement.

Understanding Key Marketing Metrics and Reports

Understanding key marketing metrics and reports is crucial for evaluating the effectiveness of your marketing efforts and making data-driven decisions. HubSpot offers a range of reports that provide insights into various aspects of your marketing strategy. Here are some essential marketing metrics and reports in HubSpot:

- Traffic and Conversion Metrics: Monitor metrics such as website visits, leads generated, conversion rates, and customer acquisitions. These metrics indicate the overall performance of your marketing campaigns.

- Email Marketing Reports: Analyze email performance metrics, including open rates, click-through rates, bounce rates, and unsubscribe rates. Use this data to optimize your email marketing strategy.
- Social Media Reports: Track social media engagement metrics, such as likes, shares, comments, and follower growth. Assess the impact of your social media efforts and identify opportunities for improvement.
- Lead Generation Reports: Evaluate the effectiveness of lead generation efforts, such as form submissions, gated content downloads, and landing page conversions. Identify high-converting lead generation assets.
- Sales Funnel Reports: Monitor the progression of leads through the sales funnel, from initial contact to closed deals. Identify areas where leads may be getting stuck and optimize your sales process accordingly.
- Customer Retention and Satisfaction: Measure customer satisfaction metrics, such as Net Promoter Score (NPS) and customer retention rates. Happy customers are more likely to become brand advocates and repeat buyers.
- Campaign Performance Reports: Assess the performance of specific marketing campaigns to determine their impact on lead generation, conversion rates, and revenue generation.
- ROI Analysis: Calculate the return on investment (ROI) for different marketing initiatives to

determine which strategies are delivering the best results.

Interpreting Data for Informed Decision Making

Interpreting data is essential for making informed decisions and optimizing your marketing strategies. In HubSpot, data interpretation involves analyzing reports, identifying trends, and drawing actionable insights. Here's how to interpret data for informed decision making:

- Set Clear Objectives: Start by defining clear objectives for your marketing initiatives. Determine what you want to achieve and the key performance indicators (KPIs) that align with your goals.
- Identify Trends and Patterns: Analyze data over time to identify trends and patterns. Look for recurring behaviors or changes in metrics that can provide valuable insights into your marketing efforts' impact.
- Compare Performance: Compare the performance of different campaigns, channels, or time periods to identify what's working and what needs improvement.
- A/B Testing Analysis: Evaluate the results of A/B tests to identify the most effective variations and apply those insights to optimize future campaigns.
- Audience Segmentation: Segment your audience based on different criteria, such as demographics, behaviors, or engagement levels. Analyze how each segment responds to your marketing efforts to tailor your approach accordingly.

- Focus on ROI: Prioritize marketing activities with a high ROI. Determine which campaigns or channels are generating the most revenue and allocate resources accordingly.
- Draw Actionable Insights: Translate data insights into actionable steps for improvement. Use data to inform your marketing strategies, content creation, and lead nurturing efforts.
- Iterate and Improve: Marketing is an iterative process. Continuously monitor and analyze data, and use insights to refine your strategies for ongoing improvement.
- Align Sales and Marketing: Collaborate with the sales team to gain insights into lead quality, conversion rates, and customer feedback. Aligning sales and marketing data can provide a holistic view of the customer journey.
- Regular Reporting: Regularly communicate data and insights to stakeholders. Use visualizations and clear explanations to make data more accessible and actionable.

In conclusion, tracking and analyzing website traffic, understanding key marketing metrics and reports, and interpreting data for informed decision making are vital components of a successful marketing strategy. HubSpot's comprehensive analytics tools provide valuable data and insights to help businesses optimize their marketing efforts, improve customer engagement, and drive growth. By leveraging data-driven decision making, businesses can adapt their strategies to meet customer needs, increase efficiency, and achieve their marketing goals.

CHAPTER THREE

*Implementing Effective
Sales Tools*

Setting Up the Sales Dashboard

Setting up the sales dashboard in HubSpot is crucial for gaining a comprehensive view of your sales team's performance and pipeline. The sales dashboard provides real-time data and insights that help sales managers and representatives track progress, identify potential bottlenecks, and make informed decisions. Here's how to set up the sales dashboard in HubSpot:

- Customizing Dashboard Layout: Access the sales dashboard by navigating to the "Sales" tab in your HubSpot dashboard. Customize the layout to display the key metrics and reports that are relevant to your team's goals.
- Adding Performance Metrics: Add performance metrics such as sales revenue, number of deals closed, deal win rate, and average deal size to the dashboard. These metrics provide a quick overview of sales team performance.
- Sales Funnel Visualization: Include a visual representation of your sales funnel, showing the number of deals at each stage. This allows sales managers to identify where leads are getting stuck

and take necessary actions to move deals forward.

- Sales Activities Tracking: Incorporate sales activities tracking, such as calls made, emails sent, and meetings scheduled. This data helps gauge the sales team's activity level and productivity.
- Goal Tracking: Set up goal tracking to monitor progress towards specific sales targets or quotas. The dashboard should display both individual and team goals for motivation and accountability.
- Reports and Insights: Add reports that provide insights into the performance of sales representatives, conversion rates, and sales cycle length. This information helps in identifying areas for improvement and optimizing sales strategies.
- Deal Forecasting: Utilize HubSpot's deal forecasting feature to predict future sales revenue based on the deals in your pipeline. This helps sales managers make informed decisions and allocate resources effectively.

Managing Deals and Sales Pipelines

Effectively managing deals and sales pipelines is essential for sales success. HubSpot's CRM provides tools to manage deals, track progress, and ensure a smooth sales process. Here's how to manage deals and sales pipelines in HubSpot:

- Deal Stages: Define clear and well-defined deal stages that align with your sales process. Customize the deal stages in HubSpot's CRM to match your specific business workflow.
- Deal Properties: Utilize deal properties to capture and store important deal information, such as

deal amount, close date, and deal owner. Custom deal properties can be created to store additional data relevant to your sales process.

- Deal Assignment: Assign deals to the appropriate sales representatives based on territory, specialization, or other criteria. This ensures that deals are routed to the right person for follow-up and management.
- Sales Pipeline View: Use HubSpot's sales pipeline view to visualize all deals in progress. Drag and drop deals into different stages as they progress through the sales cycle.
- Deal Tasks and Activities: Assign tasks and activities to deals to ensure timely follow-up and engagement with prospects. Set reminders for important follow-ups and track all interactions with the deal.
- Deal Documents and Attachments: Attach relevant documents, proposals, or quotes to deals to keep all information in one place and easily accessible.
- Deal Collaboration: Collaborate with team members by adding them as followers to deals. This allows team members to stay informed about deal progress and provide assistance when needed.
- Deal Source Tracking: Utilize HubSpot's deal source tracking to identify which marketing efforts or channels are driving the most valuable leads and deals.

Utilizing Sales Automation for Efficiency

Sales automation is a powerful tool for increasing

efficiency and productivity within the sales process. HubSpot's CRM offers various automation features to streamline repetitive tasks and focus on building relationships with prospects. Here's how to utilize sales automation in HubSpot:

- Email Templates and Sequences: Create email templates for common sales communications and use sequences to automate follow-up emails. This saves time and ensures consistent messaging.
- Meeting Scheduling: Use HubSpot's meeting scheduling tool to allow prospects to book meetings directly with sales representatives. This eliminates the back-and-forth in scheduling and improves the customer experience.
- Task Automation: Automate task creation for sales representatives based on specific triggers or actions, such as sending a follow-up email after a call or scheduling a demo after a prospect reaches a certain lead score.
- Lead Rotation: Automate lead rotation among sales representatives to ensure a fair distribution of leads and opportunities.
- Deal Stage Automation: Set up automation to move deals to different stages in the pipeline automatically. For example, a deal may move from "Prospecting" to "Qualified" after a discovery call is completed.
- Notifications and Alerts: Configure notifications and alerts for important events, such as when a deal is won or lost, when a high-priority lead submits a form, or when a key prospect engages with your website.
- Sales Documents Tracking: Use HubSpot's

document tracking feature to monitor how prospects interact with sales documents, such as proposals or contracts.

Tracking Sales Performance and Metrics

Tracking sales performance and metrics is essential for measuring success, identifying areas for improvement, and making data-driven decisions. HubSpot's CRM provides in-depth sales reports that offer valuable insights into sales performance. Here's how to track sales performance and metrics in HubSpot:

- Deal Reports: Access deal reports in the "Sales" tab to monitor key metrics, including deals won, deals lost, average deal amount, and sales pipeline value.
- Deal Forecasting Reports: Utilize deal forecasting reports to project future revenue based on deals in your sales pipeline. This assists with resource planning and goal setting.
- Sales Team Performance Reports: Analyze individual sales representatives' performance using sales team performance reports. Identify top performers and areas where additional coaching or training may be needed.
- Sales Activity Reports: Track sales activities such as calls made, emails sent, and meetings scheduled. This data provides insights into the sales team's productivity and effort.
- Deal Conversion Rates: Monitor deal conversion rates at each stage of the sales pipeline. This helps identify potential bottlenecks and areas for improvement in the sales process.

- Deal Source and Channel Reports: Determine which marketing efforts or channels are generating the most successful leads and deals. This information guides your marketing strategy and resource allocation.
- Sales Performance Dashboard: Customize your sales performance dashboard to display the most relevant and critical metrics for your team's goals and objectives.
- Historical Performance: Compare current sales performance with historical data to identify trends and track progress toward long-term goals.

By setting up the sales dashboard, effectively managing deals and sales pipelines, utilizing sales automation for efficiency, and tracking sales performance and metrics in HubSpot, businesses can optimize their sales processes, increase productivity, and achieve greater success in converting leads to customers. HubSpot's CRM provides the tools and insights needed to drive sales growth and meet revenue targets.

Integrating Customer Support And Service

Utilizing the HubSpot Service Hub

The HubSpot Service Hub is a powerful customer service and support platform that helps businesses deliver exceptional customer experiences. It enables teams to manage customer tickets, provide timely support, and gather valuable feedback. Here's how to utilize the HubSpot Service Hub effectively:

- Ticket Management: Use the Service Hub to organize and manage customer support tickets. Tickets are logged and tracked from creation to resolution, ensuring that no customer inquiry falls through the cracks.
- Knowledge Base: Create a knowledge base with self-help articles, FAQs, and guides to empower customers to find solutions to common issues on their own. This reduces the need for repetitive inquiries and improves customer satisfaction.
- Live Chat: Enable live chat on your website to offer real-time support to visitors and prospects. Live chat allows agents to engage with customers proactively, resolve issues quickly, and capture leads.
- Conversations Inbox: The Conversations Inbox consolidates all customer interactions, including email, chat, and social media messages, in one place. This streamlines communication and ensures consistent responses across channels.
- Automation and Workflows: Automate repetitive tasks and set up workflows for customer

interactions. For example, create automated responses for common inquiries or trigger follow-up actions based on customer behavior.

- Reporting and Analytics: Utilize reporting and analytics in the Service Hub to gain insights into response times, customer satisfaction scores, ticket volume, and agent performance. Use this data to identify trends and areas for improvement.
- Customer Feedback Surveys: Implement customer feedback surveys to gather valuable insights about your products, services, and support experience. This feedback helps identify strengths and weaknesses in your customer service process.

Managing Customer Tickets and Inquiries

Effectively managing customer tickets and inquiries is essential for providing timely and satisfactory support. In the HubSpot Service Hub, you can efficiently handle customer inquiries and ensure that each ticket receives the attention it deserves. Here's how to manage customer tickets and inquiries in HubSpot:

- Ticket Creation: When a customer reaches out for support via email, chat, or any other channel, create a new ticket in the Service Hub. Include all relevant details, such as the customer's name, contact information, issue description, and priority level.
- Ticket Prioritization: Set priority levels for tickets based on the urgency and impact of the issue. This helps your support team prioritize their efforts and address critical issues first.

- Ticket Assignment: Assign tickets to the appropriate support agents or teams based on their expertise and workload. This ensures that each ticket is handled by the most qualified person.
- Ticket Status Tracking: Monitor the status of each ticket throughout its lifecycle. Use custom ticket statuses to indicate if a ticket is open, in progress, pending customer response, or resolved.
- Collaboration and Internal Notes: Encourage collaboration among support agents by using internal notes within tickets. Agents can share information, updates, and insights to provide seamless support to customers.
- SLA Management: Set up Service Level Agreements (SLAs) to establish response and resolution times for different types of tickets. SLAs help maintain service quality and meet customer expectations.
- Ticket Escalation: Implement ticket escalation protocols for urgent or complex issues that require higher-level support or specialized expertise.
- Ticket Automation: Automate ticket creation, assignment, and follow-up tasks using workflows. This saves time and ensures that tickets are handled promptly and efficiently.
- Ticket Tagging and Categorization: Use tags and categories to organize and filter tickets based on common themes or issues. This allows for easy ticket routing and analysis of customer feedback.

Implementing Customer Feedback and Surveys

Customer feedback and surveys are valuable tools for understanding customer needs and improving your products and services. In the HubSpot Service Hub, you can implement customer feedback surveys to gather insights and measure customer satisfaction. Here's how to implement customer feedback and surveys in HubSpot:

- Survey Creation: Create customer feedback surveys using HubSpot's survey tool. Design surveys with a mix of multiple-choice questions, open-ended questions, and rating scales to gather comprehensive feedback.
- Net Promoter Score (NPS) Surveys: Use NPS surveys to measure customer loyalty and satisfaction. Ask customers to rate the likelihood of recommending your business to others.
- Customer Satisfaction (CSAT) Surveys: Conduct CSAT surveys to gauge customer satisfaction with specific interactions or support experiences. Ask customers to rate their satisfaction on a scale.
- Feedback Collection: Send surveys to customers at appropriate touchpoints, such as after a support interaction or after a purchase. Consider using automated workflows to trigger surveys based on specific actions or milestones.
- In-App Surveys: Implement in-app surveys to gather feedback directly within your product or website. In-app surveys offer a seamless user experience and encourage higher response rates.
- Follow-Up Actions: Based on survey responses, set up automated follow-up actions. For example, send a personalized thank-you email to customers who provide positive feedback or route negative feedback to support managers for immediate

attention.

- Analyzing Survey Results: Use HubSpot's survey reporting and analytics to interpret survey results. Identify trends, common themes, and areas for improvement in your products or support process.
- Customer Feedback Loop: Close the feedback loop by addressing customer concerns and sharing the actions taken based on their feedback. Demonstrating responsiveness to customer feedback builds trust and loyalty.
- Anonymous Surveys: Offer the option for customers to provide feedback anonymously to encourage honest responses.
- Continuous Improvement: Use customer feedback as a basis for continuous improvement in your products, services, and customer support processes. Make data-driven decisions and prioritize initiatives that align with customer needs.

By utilizing the HubSpot Service Hub, managing customer tickets and inquiries effectively, and implementing customer feedback and surveys, businesses can enhance their customer service experience, build strong customer relationships, and drive long-term loyalty and advocacy. HubSpot's comprehensive tools empower businesses to provide exceptional customer support and continuously improve their offerings based on valuable customer insights.,

Enhancing Collaboration With Hubspot

Utilizing HubSpot's Team and User Management Features

HubSpot's team and user management features allow businesses to efficiently organize and collaborate within the platform. Managing user access, roles, and permissions is essential for maintaining security and ensuring that team members have the appropriate level of access to the tools they need. Here's how to utilize HubSpot's team and user management features effectively:

- User Roles and Permissions: Assign different user roles to team members based on their responsibilities and requirements. HubSpot offers roles such as Super Admin, Marketing Admin, Sales Admin, Service Admin, and more, each with specific permissions.
- User Access Levels: Control user access to specific features and data within HubSpot by adjusting their access levels. For instance, you can limit access to sensitive data or restrict the ability to modify critical settings.
- Team Segmentation: Organize users into teams or groups based on departments or functions. This allows for easier user management and more straightforward assignment of tasks and responsibilities.
- User Onboarding: Streamline the onboarding process for new team members by providing access to relevant tools and resources. Utilize templates and documentation to guide them in understanding HubSpot's features.

- User Deactivation: Deactivate users who no longer require access to HubSpot or have left the company. This helps maintain data security and ensures that only authorized personnel have access to the platform.
- Two-Factor Authentication (2FA): Enable 2FA for an extra layer of security, requiring users to provide a second form of verification (such as a code sent to their phone) when logging into HubSpot.
- Audit Logs: Monitor user activity and changes made in the platform using HubSpot's audit logs. This helps track any suspicious actions and maintain data integrity.
- Custom User Permissions: Customize user permissions for specific scenarios that may not be covered by standard roles. This provides fine-grained control over access to certain features and data.

Collaborating on Projects and Tasks

Effective collaboration is vital for ensuring team efficiency and productivity. HubSpot provides collaboration features that allow teams to work together seamlessly on projects and tasks. Here's how to collaborate effectively in HubSpot:

- Team Dashboards: Create dashboards that provide a centralized view of project progress and key metrics. Dashboards can be customized to display data relevant to specific teams or projects.
- Task Management: Utilize HubSpot's task management tools to assign tasks, set due dates, and track progress. This ensures that team

members are aware of their responsibilities and deadlines.

- Task Notifications: Set up notifications to alert team members when tasks are assigned or due. This helps in managing workloads and ensuring timely completion of tasks.
- Comments and Notes: Use comments and notes within tasks to facilitate communication and provide updates on progress. Team members can collaborate within the task itself, streamlining communication.
- Document Sharing: Share important documents and files within HubSpot, reducing the need to switch between different tools for collaboration.
- Project Boards: Use project boards to organize tasks and projects visually. Project boards provide a clear overview of the status of different tasks and help in prioritizing work.
- Document Versioning: HubSpot's document versioning feature ensures that team members are always working on the latest version of a document, avoiding conflicts and confusion.
- @Mentions: Use @mentions in comments or notes to notify specific team members or bring their attention to a particular task or update.

Integrating HubSpot with other Team Tools

Integrating HubSpot with other team tools enhances efficiency and streamlines workflows. HubSpot offers a wide range of integrations with popular productivity and collaboration tools. Here's how to integrate HubSpot with other team tools:

- CRM Integrations: Connect HubSpot's CRM with other customer relationship management tools to ensure seamless data synchronization and a unified view of customer interactions.
- Email Integrations: Integrate HubSpot with your email client (such as Gmail or Outlook) to track email opens, clicks, and engagement within HubSpot's CRM.
- Calendar Integrations: Sync your calendar with HubSpot to schedule meetings, tasks, and follow-ups directly from the platform.
- Marketing Automation Integrations: Integrate HubSpot with marketing automation tools to align marketing efforts with sales and customer service activities.
- Project Management Integrations: Connect HubSpot with project management tools to centralize task assignment, progress tracking, and team collaboration.
- Document Collaboration Integrations: Integrate HubSpot with document collaboration platforms to simplify file sharing and collaboration on content.
- Reporting and Analytics Integrations: Connect HubSpot with reporting and analytics tools to gain deeper insights into marketing, sales, and customer service performance.
- Chat and Communication Integrations: Integrate HubSpot's chat feature with communication tools to enable real-time customer support and lead capture.

By effectively utilizing HubSpot's team and user management features, collaborating on projects and tasks, and integrating HubSpot with other team tools, businesses can create a seamless and efficient working environment. These strategies promote collaboration, improve productivity, and empower teams to achieve their goals effectively using the HubSpot platform.

CHAPTER FOUR

Advanced Tips And Tricks

Utilizing HubSpot's Team and User Management Features

HubSpot's team and user management features allow businesses to efficiently organize and collaborate within the platform. Managing user access, roles, and permissions is essential for maintaining security and ensuring that team members have the appropriate level of access to the tools they need. Here's how to utilize HubSpot's team and user management features effectively:

- User Roles and Permissions: Assign different user roles to team members based on their responsibilities and requirements. HubSpot offers roles such as Super Admin, Marketing Admin, Sales Admin, Service Admin, and more, each with specific permissions.
- User Access Levels: Control user access to specific features and data within HubSpot by adjusting their access levels. For instance, you can limit access to sensitive data or restrict the ability to modify critical settings.
- Team Segmentation: Organize users into teams or groups based on departments or functions. This allows for easier user management and more straightforward assignment of tasks and responsibilities.
- User Onboarding: Streamline the onboarding process for new team members by providing access to relevant tools and resources. Utilize templates and documentation to guide them in understanding HubSpot's features.

- User Deactivation: Deactivate users who no longer require access to HubSpot or have left the company. This helps maintain data security and ensures that only authorized personnel have access to the platform.
- Two-Factor Authentication (2FA): Enable 2FA for an extra layer of security, requiring users to provide a second form of verification (such as a code sent to their phone) when logging into HubSpot.
- Audit Logs: Monitor user activity and changes made in the platform using HubSpot's audit logs. This helps track any suspicious actions and maintain data integrity.
- Custom User Permissions: Customize user permissions for specific scenarios that may not be covered by standard roles. This provides fine-grained control over access to certain features and data.

Collaborating on Projects and Tasks

Effective collaboration is vital for ensuring team efficiency and productivity. HubSpot provides collaboration features that allow teams to work together seamlessly on projects and tasks. Here's how to collaborate effectively in HubSpot:

- Team Dashboards: Create dashboards that provide a centralized view of project progress and key metrics. Dashboards can be customized to display data relevant to specific teams or projects.
- Task Management: Utilize HubSpot's task management tools to assign tasks, set due dates, and track progress. This ensures that team

members are aware of their responsibilities and deadlines.

- Task Notifications: Set up notifications to alert team members when tasks are assigned or due. This helps in managing workloads and ensuring timely completion of tasks.
- Comments and Notes: Use comments and notes within tasks to facilitate communication and provide updates on progress. Team members can collaborate within the task itself, streamlining communication.
- Document Sharing: Share important documents and files within HubSpot, reducing the need to switch between different tools for collaboration.
- Project Boards: Use project boards to organize tasks and projects visually. Project boards provide a clear overview of the status of different tasks and help in prioritizing work.
- Document Versioning: HubSpot's document versioning feature ensures that team members are always working on the latest version of a document, avoiding conflicts and confusion.
- @Mentions: Use @mentions in comments or notes to notify specific team members or bring their attention to a particular task or update.

Integrating HubSpot with other Team Tools

Integrating HubSpot with other team tools enhances efficiency and streamlines workflows. HubSpot offers a wide range of integrations with popular productivity and collaboration tools. Here's how to integrate HubSpot with other team tools:

- CRM Integrations: Connect HubSpot's CRM with other customer relationship management tools to ensure seamless data synchronization and a unified view of customer interactions.
- Email Integrations: Integrate HubSpot with your email client (such as Gmail or Outlook) to track email opens, clicks, and engagement within HubSpot's CRM.
- Calendar Integrations: Sync your calendar with HubSpot to schedule meetings, tasks, and follow-ups directly from the platform.
- Marketing Automation Integrations: Integrate HubSpot with marketing automation tools to align marketing efforts with sales and customer service activities.
- Project Management Integrations: Connect HubSpot with project management tools to centralize task assignment, progress tracking, and team collaboration.
- Document Collaboration Integrations: Integrate HubSpot with document collaboration platforms to simplify file sharing and collaboration on content.
- Reporting and Analytics Integrations: Connect HubSpot with reporting and analytics tools to gain deeper insights into marketing, sales, and customer service performance.
- Chat and Communication Integrations: Integrate HubSpot's chat feature with communication tools to enable real-time customer support and lead capture.

By effectively utilizing HubSpot's team and user management features, collaborating on projects and tasks, and integrating HubSpot with other team tools, businesses can create a seamless and efficient working environment. These strategies promote collaboration, improve productivity, and empower teams to achieve their goals effectively using the HubSpot platform.

BEST PRACTICES FOR HUBSPOT USERS

Avoiding Common Mistakes and Pitfalls

While HubSpot offers powerful tools and capabilities, it's essential to avoid common mistakes and pitfalls that can hinder your marketing and sales efforts. By being aware of these potential challenges, you can optimize your strategies and achieve better results. Here are some common mistakes to avoid when using HubSpot:

- Incomplete Data and Segmentation: Ensure that your contact database is up-to-date and properly segmented. Incomplete or outdated data can lead to ineffective targeting and personalization.
- Neglecting Lead Nurturing: Don't focus solely on acquiring new leads; prioritize lead nurturing as well. Engage with leads throughout their buyer's journey to build trust and increase conversion rates.
- Overlooking Automation Best Practices: While automation can streamline processes, be cautious not to over-automate. Personalization and human touch are still essential in building meaningful relationships with customers.

- Ignoring Analytics: Don't neglect the data and insights available in HubSpot's reporting and analytics. Regularly review performance metrics to identify areas for improvement and optimize your strategies.
- Lack of Collaboration Between Teams: Ensure seamless collaboration between marketing, sales, and customer service teams. Alignment between departments is crucial for a cohesive customer experience.
- Neglecting Mobile Optimization: With an increasing number of users accessing content on mobile devices, ensure that your emails, landing pages, and website are mobile-responsive.
- Poorly Designed Landing Pages: Pay attention to the design and content of your landing pages. Cluttered or confusing layouts can deter visitors from taking action.
- Neglecting A/B Testing: Don't miss out on the opportunity to A/B test different elements of your campaigns. Testing can uncover insights that lead to improved performance.
- Inconsistent Content Quality: Maintain consistency in the quality and tone of your content. High-quality and valuable content fosters credibility and trust with your audience.
- Overlooking Customer Feedback: Don't underestimate the value of customer feedback. Act on feedback to address concerns and improve customer satisfaction.

Implementing Successful Marketing and Sales Workflows

Successful marketing and sales workflows are key to

driving efficient and effective processes within your organization. HubSpot's automation tools can be leveraged to optimize workflows and achieve your business goals. Here's how to implement successful marketing and sales workflows in HubSpot:

- Define Clear Goals: Clearly outline the objectives of each workflow and how they align with your overall marketing and sales strategies.
- Segment Your Audience: Use buyer personas and behavior-based segmentation to tailor workflows for different customer segments. This ensures personalized and relevant interactions.
- Automate Lead Nurturing: Design lead nurturing workflows to deliver targeted content based on the stage of the buyer's journey. Guide leads through the funnel with relevant messaging.
- Align Marketing and Sales: Create workflows that facilitate seamless handoffs between marketing and sales teams. Implement lead scoring and assign qualified leads to sales representatives.
- Monitor Performance: Regularly analyze the performance of your workflows. Track key metrics, such as conversion rates, engagement, and revenue generated.
- Continuous Optimization: Use data insights to optimize your workflows continuously. Test different approaches and make data-driven adjustments to improve results.
- Integrate with CRM: Integrate your marketing and sales workflows with HubSpot's CRM to ensure a unified view of customer interactions and streamline communication between teams.
- Prioritize Customer Experience: Keep the

customer at the center of your workflows. Focus on delivering a positive and seamless experience at every touchpoint.

Staying Up-to-date with HubSpot's Latest Features

HubSpot regularly updates its platform with new features and improvements to enhance user experience and functionality. Staying up-to-date with these changes ensures that you can leverage the latest capabilities and remain competitive in your marketing and sales efforts. Here's how to stay informed about HubSpot's latest features:

- Subscribe to Updates: Subscribe to HubSpot's blog, email newsletters, and social media channels to receive announcements about new features and updates.
- Attend Webinars and Events: Participate in HubSpot webinars and events, where they often introduce new features and provide insights into best practices.
- Join HubSpot Community: Engage with the HubSpot Community to connect with other users, share knowledge, and stay informed about updates.
- Explore the Knowledge Base: Regularly check HubSpot's Knowledge Base for articles and documentation on new features and how to use them.
- Read HubSpot Academy: HubSpot Academy offers courses and certifications that cover various aspects of the platform, including new features and updates.

- Participate in Beta Programs: HubSpot occasionally offers beta programs for new features. Participating in these programs gives you early access to features and allows you to provide feedback.
- Schedule Training Sessions: HubSpot offers training sessions that cover new features and updates. Take advantage of these sessions to learn from experts and ask questions.
- Utilize HubSpot Support: Reach out to HubSpot Support if you have questions about new features or need assistance in implementing them.

By avoiding common mistakes and pitfalls, implementing successful marketing and sales workflows, and staying up-to-date with HubSpot's latest features, you can make the most of the platform's capabilities and drive success in your marketing and sales efforts. HubSpot's robust tools and resources provide businesses with the means to deliver exceptional customer experiences and achieve their growth objectives.

Troubleshooting And Support

Handling Technical Issues and Errors

While HubSpot is a robust platform, encountering technical issues or errors is inevitable from time to time. Handling these challenges promptly and effectively is crucial to ensure smooth operations and minimize disruptions. Here's how to handle technical issues and errors in HubSpot:

- Diagnose the Issue: Start by understanding the scope and nature of the problem. Check if the issue is specific to certain pages, features, or actions within HubSpot.
- Check Status and Updates: Before troubleshooting, visit HubSpot's status page or community forums to check if there are any known issues or ongoing maintenance that could be causing the problem.
- Clear Browser Cache and Cookies: Sometimes, caching or cookie issues can cause unexpected behavior. Clear your browser's cache and cookies, then refresh the page to see if the issue persists.
- Disable Browser Extensions: Browser extensions can interfere with HubSpot's functionality. Temporarily disable extensions to check if they are causing the problem.
- Try Another Browser: If the issue persists, try accessing HubSpot from a different browser to determine if it is browser-specific.
- Check Network Connection: Ensure you have a stable internet connection to avoid disruptions or

loading issues.
- Review Recent Changes: If the issue started after making changes in HubSpot, review the recent changes to identify potential causes.
- Check HubSpot Settings: Verify that your HubSpot settings are configured correctly and are aligned with your business needs.
- Contact HubSpot Support: If the issue persists or is critical, reach out to HubSpot Support for assistance. Provide them with detailed information about the problem and any troubleshooting steps you have already taken.
- Log Support Tickets: HubSpot's Support team can assist with technical issues and errors. Log a support ticket through the HubSpot Support portal and provide as much information as possible about the problem.
- Engage with the Community: HubSpot's Community Forum is a valuable resource for seeking advice and insights from other users who may have encountered similar issues.
- Utilize Knowledge Base and Documentation: HubSpot's Knowledge Base and documentation provide step-by-step guides and troubleshooting tips for various technical challenges.

Accessing HubSpot Support and Resources

HubSpot offers a wealth of resources to help users maximize the platform's capabilities and resolve any challenges they encounter. Accessing HubSpot Support and utilizing available resources ensures that users can make the most of the platform's features. Here's how to access HubSpot Support and resources:

- HubSpot Support Portal: Access HubSpot's Support portal directly from the platform. Click on the "Help" button in the bottom right corner of the dashboard to access support options.
- Knowledge Base: HubSpot's Knowledge Base contains a vast collection of articles, tutorials, and guides that cover various aspects of the platform. Use the search function to find answers to specific questions or topics.
- HubSpot Academy: HubSpot Academy offers free courses and certifications on inbound marketing, sales, customer service, and HubSpot tools. Take advantage of these resources to expand your knowledge and expertise.
- Community Forum: Engage with the HubSpot Community Forum to connect with other users, share experiences, and seek advice. Community members often offer valuable insights and solutions to common challenges.
- HubSpot Blog: HubSpot's blog provides updates, industry insights, and best practices to help users stay informed about the latest trends and features.
- Webinars and Events: Attend HubSpot webinars and events to learn from experts, discover new features, and gain practical insights into using the platform effectively.
- HubSpot User Groups (HUGs): Join a HubSpot User Group in your area to connect with local HubSpot users, attend meetups, and share knowledge.
- HubSpot's Social Media Channels: Follow HubSpot on social media platforms for updates, announcements, and tips.

- HubSpot Support via Email or Phone: Contact HubSpot Support directly for assistance with technical issues, questions, or guidance.
- HubSpot Partner Program: If you're working with a HubSpot partner agency, leverage their expertise and support for your marketing, sales, and customer service efforts.

By accessing HubSpot Support and utilizing available resources, users can overcome challenges, enhance their proficiency with the platform, and achieve their marketing and sales objectives effectively. HubSpot's commitment to providing excellent support and a wealth of educational resources empowers businesses to succeed in their inbound marketing and customer engagement strategies.

The Future Of Hubspot And Marketing Automation

Exploring HubSpot's Roadmap and Updates

HubSpot is continuously evolving to meet the changing needs of businesses and the dynamic landscape of marketing and sales. Exploring HubSpot's roadmap and staying updated on new features and updates is essential to leverage the platform's full potential. Here's how to explore HubSpot's roadmap and stay informed about updates:

- HubSpot Product Updates Blog: HubSpot's Product Updates Blog regularly announces new features, improvements, and enhancements to the platform. Visit the blog to stay up-to-date with the latest developments.
- Release Notes: Review HubSpot's release notes to get detailed information about each update and its impact on your workflows.
- Webinars and Events: HubSpot conducts webinars and events to showcase new features and share best practices. Participate in these events to learn about the latest updates directly from HubSpot experts.
- HubSpot User Groups (HUGs): Join a HubSpot User Group to connect with other users and receive updates about the platform. Local HUG events often feature discussions on upcoming features and changes.
- Early Access Programs: Participate in early access programs to get a preview of upcoming features and provide feedback to shape their development.

- HubSpot Community Forum: Engage with the HubSpot Community Forum to discuss updates and new features with other users. Community members often share insights and experiences with the latest changes.
- HubSpot Academy: Stay updated with the latest trends and features by taking relevant courses and certifications on HubSpot Academy.
- Social Media Channels: Follow HubSpot on social media platforms to receive real-time updates, announcements, and insights from the company.
- Partner Agencies: If you work with a HubSpot partner agency, they can keep you informed about updates and how they may impact your strategies.
- HubSpot Support: HubSpot Support can provide information about updates and guide you on how to use new features effectively.

Preparing for the Future of Marketing and Sales

The landscape of marketing and sales is continually evolving, driven by technological advancements and changing consumer behaviors. Preparing for the future of marketing and sales is crucial to remain competitive and achieve sustainable growth. Here's how to prepare for the future of marketing and sales:

- Stay Agile: Embrace agility in your marketing and sales strategies to adapt quickly to changing trends and consumer preferences.
- Emphasize Personalization: Focus on personalized marketing and sales experiences to cater to individual customer needs and preferences.
- Adopt New Technologies: Stay abreast of

emerging technologies, such as artificial intelligence, chatbots, and voice search, and explore how they can enhance your marketing and sales efforts.

- Leverage Data and Analytics: Use data-driven insights to make informed decisions and optimize your marketing and sales strategies.
- Prioritize Customer Experience: Customer experience is a key differentiator in the future of marketing and sales. Focus on delivering exceptional experiences at every touchpoint.
- Invest in Content Marketing: Content will continue to play a crucial role in attracting and engaging customers. Invest in high-quality, valuable content that resonates with your target audience.
- Embrace Omnichannel Marketing: Provide a seamless experience across multiple channels and devices to engage customers wherever they are.
- Nurture Customer Relationships: Build long-term relationships with customers through effective lead nurturing and customer support.
- Focus on Sustainability and Social Responsibility: Consumers increasingly value sustainability and social responsibility. Align your marketing and sales efforts with meaningful causes.
- Continuous Learning: Encourage a culture of continuous learning within your marketing and sales teams. Stay updated with industry trends and best practices to remain competitive.
- Collaborate Across Departments: Foster collaboration between marketing, sales, and customer service teams to provide a unified and

cohesive customer experience.

- Adapt to Regulatory Changes: Stay informed about changes in data privacy regulations and ensure compliance with relevant laws.

By exploring HubSpot's roadmap and updates and preparing for the future of marketing and sales, businesses can position themselves for success in a rapidly evolving marketplace. Embracing innovation, personalization, and customer-centricity will be essential to thrive in the future landscape of marketing and sales

CONCLUSION

In conclusion, "The Simplified HubSpot User Guide" offers readers a comprehensive and user-friendly journey into the world of HubSpot's powerful marketing and sales automation platform. Throughout this book, we have explored the fundamental features and functionalities that can transform businesses, helping them reach new heights of success and growth.

As you close this guide, I encourage you to embrace the knowledge gained and implement it effectively in your marketing and sales strategies. HubSpot's intuitive interface and wide array of tools are designed to streamline processes, enhance customer interactions, and boost overall productivity.

Remember, success with HubSpot lies not only in mastering the tools but also in fostering a customer-centric approach and cultivating meaningful relationships with your audience. By leveraging the insights and strategies shared in this book, you can build lasting connections and nurture leads into loyal customers.

In your journey with HubSpot, continuous learning and adaptation are key. As the platform evolves, so too will your understanding of its potential. Stay curious, stay open to experimentation, and stay committed to refining your marketing and sales efforts for optimal results.

Ultimately, "The Simplified HubSpot User Guide" aims to

empower you to take charge of your marketing and sales endeavors, making data-driven decisions, and achieving sustainable growth. May this book serve as a valuable resource and a source of inspiration as you navigate the dynamic landscape of digital marketing and sales automation.

Thank you for embarking on this educational journey with us, and here's to your continued success with HubSpot